THE
LAST DAYS IN ENGLAND
OF THE
RAJAH RAMMOHUN ROY

HE

LAST DAYS IN ENGLAND
OF THE
RAJAH RAMMOHUN ROY

MARY CARPENTER

GYAN

Published by

GYAN

Gyan Publishing House
5, Ansari Road
Daryaganj, New Delhi-110002
Phone: 011-47034999, 9811692060
E-mail: books@gyanbooks.com

Distribution Network
gyanbooks.com
India, USA, Canada, UK, Australia, France

ISBN : 978-81-212-9234-4 (PB)
First Published, 1915

2nd Impression 2023

Printed at: Gyan Press, Delhi.

THE LAST DAYS IN ENGLAND OF THE RAJAH RAMMOHUN ROY
Author: MARY CARPENTER

RAJA RAM MOHAN RAY.

From a painting by Briggs in the Bristol Philosophical Institution

THE LAST DAYS IN ENGLAND OF THE RAJAH RAMMOHUN ROY.

BY

MARY CARPENTER

OF

BRISTOL,

AUTHOR OF "OUR CONVICTS" "MORNING AND EVENING MEDITATIONS," "SIX MONTHS IN INDIA," ETC., ETC.

(ILLUSTRATED).

PUBLISHED

BY

THE RAMMOHUN LIBRARY AND FREE READING-ROOM,

267, UPPER CIRCULAR ROAD,

CALCUTTA.

1915.

TO THE COUNTRYMEN

OF

THE RAJAH RAMMOHUN ROY,

WHO,

EMANCIPATING THEMSELVES FROM THE THRALDOM

OF IDOLATRY AND SUPERSTITION,

HAVE DEVOTED THEMSELVES

TO PROMOTE THE ELEVATION OF THEIR COUNTRY,

THIS WORK IS INSCRIBED

BY THE EDITOR.

Preface.

TO THE FIRST EDITION.

THE Rajah RAMMOHUM ROY was, in the land of his birth a man greatly before his age. He was a light shining in thick darkness,—palpable,—impenetrable by its rays;—its lustre served only to make the surrounding gloom more visible. Hence he was appreciated during his life by very few of his countrymen, and his death appeared at the time to excite but little regret in India. It was to England that he turned for encouragement, sympathy and help, for Englishmen had shown that they comprehended in some degree the greatness of his spirit, and admired the purity and devotedness of his life. From England, therefore, he sought for aid in his efforts to regenerate his country;—he hoped after visiting her shores, and gathering strength from communion with the wise and good among her citizens, to return to India, armed with fresh power, guided by new light to accomplish the great purpose of his life.

It was otherwise ordered, for the fit time was not come. His earthly warfare was accomplished; —he was permitted to retire from the battle of life, and to lie down to rest where all that was mortal of him would be regarded as a sacred deposit, and where the memorials of his spirit would be honoured and cherished. Long years required to roll by, and many changes to take place in India, before his country should be prepared truly to appreciate the great Reformer.

More than a quarter of a century has now passed and the name of RAMMOHUN ROY begins to be reverenced as it ought to be in his native country. The seed which he sowed was long in germinating, but it never lost its vitality. He who had scattered it with no sparing hand, whether in the highways, in stray places, among thorns and brambles, or in good ground, was not permitted even to see it spring up, but having faithfully done his work, left it in charge of the Great Husbandman. The seed has sprung up and grown, man knoweth not how, "for the earth.. bringeth forth fruit of herself, first the blade, then the ear, after that the full corn in the ear." While but a very few rallied around their great Reformer in his unwearied efforts to draw away his countrymen from idolatry and superstition, and but one temple then rose among the Hindoos dedicated to the pure worship of one only God,—now there are thousands, and perhaps even tens of thousands who have emancipated themselves from the thraldom of idolatry and superstition, and in many houses of worship is proclaimed "the Fatherhood of God and the Brotherhood of Man."

The progress of improvement and the chain of events, linked together by the unerring hand of the Supreme Ruler, has led several of RAMMOHUN ROY'S countrymen to follow his example and to visit our shores. Many young Hindoos have come to England to become acquainted with English men and women in their private and public work, and in their homes,—to study our laws and our institutions,—and thus to qualify themselves on their return to India to transplant there what they have found most deserving of imitation among us. It is at the request of some of them that this volume has been prepared. The privilege of paying such a tribute to the memory of so noble and excellent a man, is highly valued by one who knew him personally, and who has always treasured with reverence the recollection not only of his devoted efforts in the cause of religion and virtue, but of his estimable qualities and purity of life. She regrets that she cannot make this work more worthy of him, from causes which will appear in the course of the narrative; she hopes, however, that this volume will be kindly received both by his countrymen, and by those who respect his name in England, and that its very deficiencies may give rise to a more complete memoir of him, and lead to a greater knowledge of his works. For this his countrymen are now prepared. The following words of one of them express the sentiments of all who know and respect their greatest man, the Rajah RAMMOHUN ROY :—

"It is now more than fifty years, that, in Bengal, there arose a genius, like a solitary star in a night of darkness, who, in spite of great opposition and persecution, gave the death blow to gross idolatry and superstition, which had degenerated the great Hindoo nation. When we consider the debased state of religion and society in those days, we find that RAMMOHUN ROY was one of those men who have made their appearance from time to time in this world to be the enlighteners of nations, and to protect men from forsaking truth. We can trace the infinite wisdom and mercy* of Providence in the fact, that at times, when nations sink in vice and error, individual men are sent, who, by the force of their intellect, the purity of their charac ter, and the earnestness of their motives, succeed in bringing men to the paths of virtue and right-eousness. In order to judge rightly of such men, we should carefully consider the times in which they lived, the state of society in which they were brought up, and the obstacles and difficulties which surrounded them;—thus we find RAM-MOHUN ROY to have been, not only a great and good man, but one whom future generations of his countrymen must regard as the FIRST HINDOO REFORMER."

Preface

TO THE SECOND EDITION.

THE first edition of this work was prepared on the eve of the Author's first visit to India, in 1866. It was hoped that its appearance would stimulate to efforts among the countrymen of the Rajah RAMMOHUN ROY to collect such material as might lead to the preparation of a complete Memoir of one of the most remarkable men and distinguished Reformers whom India and the world has ever produced. These hopes have been disappointed. The time does not appear to have yet arrived when his life and work are fully appreciated in his own country. His works have not been collected and published, and the important evidence which he gave before Parliament still lies entombed in the blue folios. Yet the seed he sowed on an apparently uncongenial soil is now springing up in every part of the country. The results he anticipated from English education have been verified. The claims of the female sex, which he so nobly supported, are being extensively acknowledged, and the general progress which has been made in his country during the forty years which have elapsed since his departure, has been far greater than he would have dared to predict. His name should not be forgotten, and imperfect as this small volume is, the present edition of it is respectfully offered to his countrymen, in the hope that it may help to keep alive the memory of the great Reformer, and lead to the publication of his works with a complete memoir.

Preface

TO THE THIRD EDITION.

The Second Edition of this book was published in London as long ago as 1875 and since the death of Miss MARY CARPENTER, no attempts have been made either in England or in India to bring out a new edition. The author of the book has certainly done a great public service by publishing this book and we think she has left a legacy which our countrymen ought to cherish with sincere love and admiration. It has been very properly remarked that the RAJAH RAMMOHUN ROY was born very much before his time. The interest which is now manifested by our countrymen in the study of the RAJAH'S life and teachings justifies our undertaking the reprint of this most interesting book and presenting it before the public after such a long period. It contains not only a faithful account but many remarkable annecdotes of the last days in the life of this epoch-making man. India is now passing through a period of transition and it is our firm conviction that a careful study of the life and teachings of the "Maker of Modern India" will help, in a large measure, the solution of many difficult problems,—social, political, religious, and educational. The authorities of the Rammohun Library and Free Reading-Room, Calcutta, who aim at perpetuating the memory of the great man, feel proud to be associated with the publication of this Third Edition. When the second edition was published, the author expressed her disappointment that the time had not come for a true appreciation of the life and work of the RAJAH by his countrymen. Since then, over 40 years have passed and many great changes have taken place in the political, social and religious thoughts of India. It is a matter of great satisfaction for us to be able to say that the RAJAH's countrymen have now begun to slowly appreciate his worth. His works have been collected and published and the people have been showing a keen desire to understand his true character and the significance of his many-sided views.

In the present edition, we have given a tri-colour portrait of (1) the RAJAH which is a copy taken from the original painting in the Bristol Philosophical

Institution by Briggs R. A, and half-tone pictures of (2) The Rammohun Memorial Hall and Library in Upper-Circular Road, Calcutta; (3) Raja Rammohun Roy's Calcutta residence in Upper Circular Road; (4) Miss Mary Carpenter; (5) an Autograph letter of the Raja while in England to his eldest son Radhaprosad Roy; (6) Death-Mask of the Raja (kindly presented to us by the late Mr. A. M. Bose's sons.); (7) Fac simile of Funeral Document; (8) Tomb of the Raja in Arno's Vale Cemetry and (9) Prince Dwarka Nath Tagore. We trust these illustrations will prove interesting to the readers.

In this Edition, we have also added a short Biographical sketch of the author of the Book and an extract from the "Visitors' Book" of the Raja's Tomb at Bristol, in Appendices G & H. We regret we cannot give an up-to-date list of the names of Indian visitors who paid their respects to the last remains of the great man. We have asked our friend Mr. P. Banerjea, M. A., who is now studying in England, to supply this gap and it is hoped that in the next edition we shall be able to include this. In addition to these, we have included in Appendix I, a criticism on this book from the pen of the Late Babu Kissory Chand Mittra—the renowned Bengalle journalist and writer—which appeared in the "*Calcutta Review*" in 1866, from which our readers will see how Rajah Rammohun Roy's religious views have been vindicated. We veuture to commend to the special attention of the readers that part of the criticism which refers to the religious convictions of the great Hindu Reformer. We are indebted to our friend Mr. Manmatha Nath Ghosh, M. A. F. S. S., F. R. E. S., for this material. In conclusion, we may take the opportunity of expressing our deep sense of obligation to Messrs. U. Roy & Sons, the celebrated Artists of Calcutta, for the assistance rendered to us in the preparation of the various blocks included in this book. We are also indebted to Mr. Sasipada Banerjee of the "Devalaya" and Mr. Hemachandra Ghosha of the Department of Land Records, Bengal for their many valuable suggestions.

The entire sale-proceeds of the present edition of this book will go towards the Building Fund of the Rammohun Library and Free Reading-Room, Calcutta.

RAMMOHUN LIBRARY,
267, Upper Circular Road,
Calcutta, January, 1, 1915.

D. N. PAL,
Honorary Secretary.

Contents.

BIOGRAPHICAL SKETCH,—p 1.

AUTOBIOGRAPHICAL SKETCH,—p. 22.

CHAPTER I.

ENGLISH IMPRESSIONS,—p. 27.

Missionary Reports, p. 33. R. Roy's Writings, p. 38. Abbé Gregoire's Pamphlet, p. 48. Testimonies to R. Roy, p. 54. R. Roy's letters, p. 60.

CHAPTER II.

ARRIVAL IN ENGLAND AND RESIDENCE IN LONDON,—p. 74.

Interview with W. Roscoe, p. 79. Arrival in London, p. 86. Reception at the Unitarian Association Meeting, p. 92. Efforts for the Elevation of Women, p. 101. Papers given to the Select Committee of the House of Commons on India, p. 112. R. Roy's publications, p. 119. Social Intercourse, p. 121. Letters to Miss Kiddell, p. 135.

CHAPTER III.

VISIT TO BRISTOL.

THE RAJAH'S DEATH AND INTERMENT,—p. 146.

Stapleton Grove, p. 146. Opinions and letters of John Foster, p. 150. Dr. Jerrard's letter, 156. Mr. Estlin's Journal, p. 158. The Rajah's Death, p. 166. Interment, p. 169. Sonnets, p. 182,

CHAPTER IV.

TRIBUTES TO THE RAJAH'S MEMORY,—p. 185.
Testimony of Mr. Hare's Family, p. 186. Miss Aikin's Letter, p. 193. Dr. Boott's Letter, p. 194. Poetical Tributes, p. 202, Tributes from his Countrymen, p. 206.

CHAPTER V.

CONCLUSION.—209.

APPENDICES.—p. 219.

LIST OF ILLUSTRATIONS.

1. Raja Rammohun Roy. Frontispiece.
2. Rammohun Roy Memorial Hall and Library in Calcutta. Page 1.
3. Raja Rammohun Roy's Calcutta Residence. " 6.
4. Miss Mary Carpenter. " 27.
5. A Letter from Raja Rammohun Roy Dated 22nd Sep. 1832, to His Eldest Son Radhaprosad Roy. " 134.
6. Death-Mask of Raja Rammohun Roy. " 197.
7. Fac simile of Funeral Document. " 169.
8. Tomb of Raja Rammohun Roy, at Arno's Vale Cemetry. " 203.
9. Prince Dwaroka Nath Tagore. " 207

A

BIOGRAPHICAL SKETCH

OF THE

RAJAH RAMMOHUN ROY,

BY THE LATE

REV. DR. LANT CARPENTER,

OF BRISTOL.

Rammohun Library and Free Reading Room, Calcutta.

U. RAY & SONS.

Biographical Sketch.

THIS volume has been prepared solely to embody what is known of the closing period of Rajah RAMMOHUN ROY'S life, which was spent in England. To do more would have been out of the Author's power. It will however be interesting to the readers to peruse the following brief Memoir, which was prepared by Rev. Dr. CARPENTER shortly after the Rajah's death, from authentic sources of information [chiefly found in the "Monthly Repository of Theology and General Literature," Vols. XIII. to XX.] ; from the Memoir prefixed to the "Precepts of Jesus," by Rev. Dr. T. REES ; from communications received from the family with whom the Rajah resided in London, and from the Rajah personally.

RAMMOHUN ROY, was the son of RAM KHANT ROY. His grandfather resided at Moorshedabad, and filled some important offices under the Moguls ; but being ill-treated by them towards the end of his life, the son took up his abode in the district of Burdwan, where he had landed property. There RAMMOHUN ROY was born, most probably about 1774. Under his father's roof he received the elements of native education, and also acquired the Persian language. He was afterwards sent to Patna to learn Arabic; and lastly to Benares to obtain a knowledge of Sanscrit, the sacred language of the Hindoos. His masters at Patna set him to study Arabic translations of some of the writings of Aristotle and Euclid; it is probable that the training thus given strengthened his mind in acuteness and close reasoning, while the knowledge which he acquired of the Mahommedan religion from Mussulmen whom he esteemed, contributed to cause that searching examination of the faith in which he was educated, which led him eventually to the important efforts he made to restore it to its early simplicity.

His family was Brahminical, of high respectability; and, of course, he was a Brahmin by birth. After his death the thread of his caste was seen round him, passing over his left shoulder and under his right. His father trained him in the doctrines of his sect; but he very early observed the diversities of opinion existing even among the idolators; and that while some exalted Brahma, the Creator, others gave the ascendancy to Vishnu, the Preserver; and others again to Siva, the

Destroyer. It is scarcely possible, too, but that his mind must have been struck by the simplicity of the Mahommedan faith and worship; and at any rate it early revolted from the frivolous or disgusting rites and ceremonies of Hindoo idolatry. Without disputing the authority of his father, he often sought from him information as to the reasons of his faith. He obtained no satisfaction; and he at last determined, at the early age of fifteen, to leave the paternal home, and to sojourn for a time in Thibet, that he might see another form of religious faith. He spent two or three years in that country, and often excited the anger of the worshippers of the Lama by his rejection of their doctrine that this pretended deity—a living man—was the creator and preserver of the world. In these circumstances he experienced the soothing kindness of the female part of the family; and his gentle, feeling heart dwelt, with deep interest, at the distance of more than forty years, on the recollection of that period; these, he said, had made him always feel respect and gratitude towards the female sex, and they doubtless contributed to that unvarying and refined courtesy which marked his intercourse with them in this country.

When he returned to Hindostan, he was met by a deputation from his father, and received by him with great consideration. He appears, from that time, to have devoted himself to the study of Sanscrit and other languages, and of the ancient books of the Hindoos. He had frequent discussions with his father: through awe of him, however, he never avowed the scepticism which he entertained as to the present forms of their religion ; but from some indirect reproaches he received, he imagined that he had fallen under his father's suspicions. His father had given him, for that country, a very superior education ; but having been brought up himself in the midst of the Mussulman Court, he appears to have thought principally of those qualifications which would recommend his son to the ancient conquerors of India. Till manhood, RAMMOHUN ROY knew very little of the English language, and that little he taught himself.

"At the age of twenty-two," says the Editor of the English Edition of the Abridgment of the Vedant and the Cena Upanished, "he commenced the study of the English language, which not pursuing with application, he five years afterwards, when I became acquainted with him, could merely speak it well enough to be understood upon the most common topics of discourse ; but could not write it with any degree of correctness. He was afterwards employed as Dewan, or principal native officer, in the collection of the revenues, in the district of which I was for five years Collector in the East India Company's Civil Service. By perusing all my public correspondence with diligence and attention, as well as by corresponding and conversing with European gentlemen, he acquired so correct a knowledge of the English language as to be enabled to write and speak in with considerable accuracy"

The father, RAM KHANT ROY, died about 1804 or 1805, having two years previously divided his property among his three sons. It was not long before RAMMOHUN ROY became the only survivor; and he thereby possessed considerable property. From this period he appears to have commenced his plans of reforming the religion of his countrymen; and in the progress of his efforts to enlighten them he must have expended large sums of money, for he gratuitously distributed most of the works which he published for the purpose. He now quitted Burdwan and removed to Moorshedabad, where he published in Persian, with an Arabic preface, a work entitled "*Against the Idolatry of all Religions.*" No one undertook to refute this book, but it raised up against, him a host of enemies, and in 1814 he retired to Calcutta, where he applied himself to the study of the English language both by reading and by conversation; he also acquired some knowledge of Latin, and paid much attention to mathematics. At this time he purchased a garden with a house constructed in the European style, in the Circular Road, at the eastern extremity of the city ; and he gradually gathered round him inquiring intelligent Hindoos, of rank and opulence, some of whom united as early as 1818 in a species of monotheistic worship.

The body of Hindoo theology is comprised in the Veds, which are writings of very high antiquity, very copious, but obscure in style ; and about two thousand years ago, VYAS drew up a compendious abstract of the whole, accompanied with explanations of the more difficult passages. This digest VYAS called the Vedant, or the Resolution of all the Veds. One portion of this respects the ritual, and another, the principles of religion. It is written in the Sanscrit language. RAMMOHUN ROY translated it into the Bengalee and Hindoostanee languages, for the benefit of his countrymen ; and afterwards published an abridgment of it, for gratuitous and extensive distribution. Of this abridgment he published an English translation in 1816, the title of which represents the Vedant as "the most celebrated and revered work of Brahminical theology, establishing the unity of the Supreme Being, and that he alone is the object of propitiation and worship." Towards the close of his preface he thus writes—"My constant reflec-

Raja Rammohun Roy's Residence, 113, Upper Circular Road, Calcutta.

U. RAY & SONS

Raja Rammohun Roy's Residence, 113, Upper Circular Road, Calcutta.

U. RAY & SONS

tions on the inconvenient, or, rather, injurious rites introduced by the peculiar practice of Hindoo idolatry, which more than any other Pagan worship destroys the texture of society—together with compassion for my countrymen—have compelled me to use every possible effort to awaken them from their dream of error; and by making them acquainted with the [their] scriptures, enable them to contemplate, with true devotion, the unity and omnipresence of nature's God. By taking the path which conscience and sincerity direct, I, born a Brahmin, have exposed myself to the complainings and reproaches even of some of my relations, whose prejudices are strong, and whose temporal advantage depends on the present system. But these, however accumulated, I can tranquilly bear; trusting that a day will arrive when my humble endeavours will be viewed with justice—perhaps acknowledged with gratitude. At any rate, whatever men may say, I cannot be deprived of this consolation—my motives are acceptable to that Being who beholds in secret and compensates openly."

After the publication of the Vedant, RAMMOHUN ROY printed in Bengalee and in English, some of the principal chapters of the Veds. The first of the series was published in 1816, and is entitled "A Translation of the Ceña Upanishad, one of the

Chapters of the Sama Veda, according to the gloss of the celebrated Shancharacarya ; establishing the Unity and Sole Omnipotence of the Supreme Being, and that He alone is the object of Worship." This was prefixed to a reprint of the Abridgment of the Vedant, published in London, in 1817, by some one who had enjoyed personal intimacy with him. The English preface contains a letter from RAMMOHUN ROY to this gentleman, which shows how well he had, even at that time, overcome the difficulties of the English language. "The consequence of my long and uninterrupted researches into religious truth (he says in this letter) has been, that I have found the doctrines of Christ more conducive to moral principles, and better adapted for the use of rational beings, than any other which have come to my knowledge ; and have also found Hindoos in general more superstitious and miserable, both in performance of their religious rites and in their domestic concerns, than the rest of the known nations of the earth." He then proceeds to state what he had done in order to render them "more happy and comfortable both here and hereafter ;." and adds, "I, however, in the beginning of my pursuits, met with the greatest opposition from their self-interested leaders, the Brahmins, and was deserted by my nearest relations ; and I consequently felt extremely melancholy. In that critical situation, the only comfort that I had was the consoling and rational conversation of my European friends, especially those of Scotland and England." In that same letter he expresses his full expectation of speedily setting off for England; but says that he had been prevented from proceeding so soon as he could wish, by the spread of his views, and the inclination manifested by many to seek for truth.

It is not surprising that the interested advocates for heathen worship should endeavour to uphold it by imputations on the character of the Reformer; and some one did publicly charge him with "rashness, self-conceit, arrogance, and impiety." Every member of his own family opposed him; and he experienced even the bitter alienation of his mother, through the influence of the interested persons around her. In his early days, his mother was a woman of fine understanding; but, through the influence of superstitious bigotry, she had been among his most bitter opponents. He, however, manifested a warm and affectionate attachment towards her, and it was with a glistening eye that he told us she had "repented" of her conduct towards him. Though convinced that his doctrines were true, she could not throw off the shackles of idolatrous customs. "RAMMOHUN," she said to him, before she set out on her last pilgrimage to Juggernath, where she died, "you are right, but I am a weak woman, and am grown too old to give up these observances, which are a comfort to me." She maintained them with the most self-denying devotion. She would not allow a female servant to accompany her; or any other provision to be made for her comfort or even support on her journey; and when at Juggernaut, she engaged in sweeping the temple of the idol. There she spent the remainder of her life—nearly a year if not more; and there she died. He recently stated, however, that before her death she expressed her great sorrow for what had passed, and declared her conviction in the unity of God, and the futility of Hindoo superstition.

D' ACOSTA, the editor of a journal at Calcutta, transmitted to the Abbe GREGOIRE, in 1818, the various publications of this extraordinary man, with some account of his history; and through GREGOIRE, RAMMOHUN ROY became extensively known and highly appreciated in France. D'ACOSTA says, that he carefully avoided every thing that could afford a pretext for excluding him from his caste, since, as a Brahmin, it was his acknowledged duty to instruct his countrymen in the sense and real commands of their sacred books. He speaks of him as distinguished in his controversy more by his logical mode of reasoning than by his general views, though far from deficient in philosophy or information. He says that all his conversation, his actions, and his manners evince a powerful sentiment of individual dignity, while, in general, meanness and feebleness of mind are characteristic of the Hindoo, and that his ingenious conversation often shows, in a strain half serious and half sportive, all that he wished to be able to do for his country. As to his personal exterior at that period, D'ACOSTA says,—"He is tall and robust; his regular features, and habitually grave countenance assume a most pleasing appearance when he is animated; he appears to have a slight disposition to melancholy." "The moderation," adds Abbe GREGOIRE, "with which he repels the attacks on his writings, the force of his arguments, and his profound knowledge of the sacred books of the Hindoos, are proofs of his fitness for the work he has undertaken; and the pecuniary sacrifices he has made, show a disinterestedness which cannot be encouraged or admired too warmly"

It was about this period that Lieut-Col, FITZCLARENCE, now the Earl of MUNSTER, became acquainted with RAMMOHUN ROY. He speaks highly of this "most extraordinary" Brahmin, of his talents and learning, his intimate knowledge of our language and eloquence in the use of it, his extensive acquaintance with our literature as well as with the Arabic and Sanscrit, his clear intelligence of the politics of Europe, and especially of England, of his fine person, and most courtly manners. The representations of the Earl indicate the amazing extent, tenaciousness, and accuracy of his memory; and in this and other respects fully accord with what we learn of him from other sources; the Author was, however, mistaken in supposing that he had been "declared to have lost caste." RAMMOHUN ROY recently stated that every effort had been made for the purpose, and that he had had, at an enormous expense, to defend himself against a series of legal proceedings instituted for the purpose of depriving him of caste, and thereby of his patrimonial inheritance. Through his profound acquaintance, however, with the Hindoo law, he baffled the efforts of his interested enemies, and proved in the Courts of justice that he had not forfeited his rights. These legal proceedings must have continued, in different ways, for several years. They appear to have terminated in the Provincial Court no long time before RAMMOHUN ROY set out for England. On leaving Calcutta, he charged his two sons to forget the conduct of their cousins in connection with them.

Besides essentially contributing to the establishment and maintenance of native schools, RAMMOHUN ROY directed his efforts, and with great success towards the extinction of the practice of burning widows. One of his tracts on this subject he dedicated to the Marchioness of HASTINGS, when the Marquis was Governor-General.

It has already been shown that as early as 1817 he had directed his attention to the Christian religion ; but he found himself greatly perplexed by the various doctrines which he saw insisted upon as essential to Christianity, in the writings of Christian authors, and in conversation with those Christian teachers with whom he had communication : he resolved, therefore, to study the original Scriptures for himself ; and for this purpose he acquired the knowledge of the Hebrew and Greek languages. Becoming strongly impressed with the excellence and importance of the Christian system of morality, he published, in 1820, in English, Sanscrit, and Bengalee, a series of selections, principally from the first three Gospels, which he entitled, "The Precepts of Jesus, the Guide to Peace and Happiness." He passed by those portions of the Evangelists which have been made the basis of distinctive doctrines ; and also (except where closely interwoven with the discourses of Christ) the narratives of miracles—believing these to be less fitted to affect the convictions of his countrymen, while the preceptive part he deemed most likely "to produce the desirable effect of improving the hearts and minds of men of different persuations and degrees of understanding." "This simple code of religion and morality," he says, at the close of his preface, "is so admirably calculated to elevate men's ideas to high and liberal notions of one God, who has equally subjected all living creatures, without distinction of caste, rank or wealth, to change, disappointment, pain and death, and has equally admitted all to be partakers of the bountiful mercies which he has lavished over nature; and is also so well fitted to regulate the conduct of the human race in the discharge of their various duties to God, to themselves, and to society; that I cannot but hope the best effects from its promulgation in the present form."

This work was published anonymously, but without concealment of the source. It brought upon him some severe and unexpected animadversions in "The Friend of India"; the writer of which uncourteously, as well as most unjustly, spoke of the Compiler as a *heathen.* Under the designation of "A Friend to Truth," RAMMOHUN ROY published an appeal to the Christian public in defence of the "Precepts of Jesus"; in which he declares, that the expressions employed in the preface should have shown the opponent "that the Compiler believed, not only in one God, whose nature and essence is beyond human comprehension, but in the truths revealed in the Christian system." He further maintains that the "Precepts of Jesus" contain not only the essence of all that is necessary to instruct mankind in their civil duties, but also the best and only means of obtaining the forgiveness of our sins, the favor of God, and strength to overcome our passions and to keep his commandments." He defends the system which the Compiler had adopted to introduce Christianity to the native inhabitants, by appealing to the fact that nearly three-fifths are Hindoos and two-fifths Mussulmans, the latter devoted from their infancy to the belief in one God ; and declares that, from his own experience in religious controversy with them, he is satisfied that he was rendering them most service by making them acquainted with those precepts (by which he appears to have meant, more generally, *instructions*) "the obedience to which he believed most peculiarly required of a Christian, and such as could by no means tend in doctrine to excite the religious horror of the Mahommedans, or the scoffs of the Hindoos." "Such dogmas or doctrinal and other passages," he afterwards says, "as are not exposed to those objections, and are not unfamiliar to the minds of those for whose benefit the compilation was intended, are generally included, in conformity with the avowed plan of the work; particularly such as seem calculated to direct our love and obedience to the beneficent Author of the universe and to him whom he graciously sent to deliver those precepts of religion and morality whose tendency is to promote universal peace and harmony." When replying to the objections of the Reviewer, that the precepts of Christ do not shew how to obtain the forgiveness of sins and the favor of God, the Friend of Truth extracts from the compilation "a few passages of that greatest of all prophets who was sent to call sinners to repentance"; and adds; "Numerous passages of the Old and New Testaments to the same effect, which might fill a volume, distinctly promise us that the forgiveness of God and the favor of his Divine Majesty may be obtained by sincere repentance, as required of sinners by the Redeemer."

On these anonymous publications, Dr. MARSHMAN, of Serampore College, published a series of animadversions which led to a very remarkable reply from RAMMOHUN ROY—the Second Appeal—with his name prefixed, which is distinguished by the closeness of his reasonings, the extent and critical accuracy of his scriptural knowledge, the comprehensiveness of his investigations, the judiciousness of his arrangement, the lucid statement of his own opinions, and the acuteness and skill with which he controverts the positions of his opponents. All the publications of this controversy were soon reprinted in London; and those who wish to become acquainted with the sentiments of this remarkable man, as to his Christian belief generally, and his own opinions respecting God and Christ, may be referred with confidence, and in an especial manner, to this Second Appeal to the Christian Public in defence of the "Precepts of Jesus." The doctrine maintained in it respecting God, is thus stated by himself:—"That the Omnipotent God, who is the only proper object of religious veneration, is one and undivided in person"; that "in reliance on numerous promises found in the sacred writings, we ought to entertain every hope of enjoying the blessings of pardon from the merciful Father, through repentance, which is declared the only means of procuring forgiveness for our failures"; and that he leads "such as worship him in spirit to righteous conduct, and ultimately to salvation, through his guiding influence which is called the Holy Spirit," "given as the consequence of their sincere prayer and supplication." And respecting "Jesus of Nazareth" he speaks as the "Christ of God": he says he places "implicit confidence" in his "veracity, candour, and perfection": he represents him as "a Being in whom dwelt all truth, and who was sent with a divine law to guide mankind by his preaching and example"; as receiving from the Father, "the commission to come into the world for the salvation of mankind"; as judging the world by the wisdom of God; as being "empowered to perform wonderful works"; he speaks of his subordinate nature and receiving all the powers which he manifested. from the Father; but also of his being "superior even to the angels in heaven, living from the beginning of the world to eternity"; and of the Father's creating "all things by him and for him"; and he dwells with great satisfaction (pp. 162—167) on the conclusion to which the instructions of Christ had led him, that the "unity existing between the Father and himself," is "a subsisting concord of will and design, such as existed among his Apostles, and not identity of being." "Had not experience (he concludes) too clearly proved that such metaphorical expressions, when taken singly and without attention to their contexts, may be made the foundation of doctrines quite at variance with the tenor of the rest of the Scriptures, I should have had no hesitation in submitting indiscriminately the whole of the doctrines of the New Testament to my countrymen; as I should have felt no apprehension that even the most ignorant of them, if left to the guidance of their own unprejudiced views of the matter, could misconceive the clear and distinct assertions they every where contain, of the unity of God and the subordinate nature of his messenger Jesus Christ."

The Second Appeal called forth another work from Dr. MARSHMAN; to which RAMMOHUN ROY published a reply in 1823, under the title of the Final Appeal. His preceding works had been printed at the Baptist Missionary Press; but the acting proprietor declined, "although in the politest manner possible," to print the Final Appeal; and RAMMOHUN ROY purchased type, and commenced an independent printing press for this and other similar publications. The imprint is "Calcutta: printed at the Unitarian Press, Dhurmtollah." He depended chiefly on native aid; and in consequence the original work has many errata. In the Preface he states that this controversy had prevented other publications which he had projected for his countrymen, as well as drawn him for three years from other literary pursuits; and that it had caused much coolness towards him in the demeanour of some whose friendship he held very dear; nevertheless, that he did not wish he had pursued a different course, since, he says, "whatever may be the opinion of the world, my own conscience fully approves of my past endeavours to defend what I esteem the cause of truth."

The Editor of the *Indian Gazette*, in adverting to this discussion, and to the other labours of this distinguished native, thus writes—"We say distinguished, because he is so among his own people, by caste, rank, and respectability; and among all men he must ever be distinguished for his philanthropy, his great learning, and his intellectual ascendancy in general." As to the controversy arising from the Precepts of Jesus, the Editor says that whatever other effects it may have caused, "it still further exhibited the acuteness of his mind, the logical power of his intellect, and the unrivalled good temper with which he could argue:" it roused up "a most gigantic combatant in the theological field—a combatant who, we are constrained to say, has not yet met with his match here."

To the public testimonies already adduced, may be added that of the celebrated SISMONDI, who, in an article in the Revue Encyclopédique for 1824, after some important observations respecting the institution of castes and the sacrifice of widows, thus proceeds: "A glorious reform has, however, begun to spread among the Hindoos. A Brahmin, whom those who know India agree in representing as one of the most virtuous and enlightened of men, RAMMOHUN ROY, is exerting himself to restore his countrymen to the worship of the true God, and to the union of morality and religion. His flock is small, but increases continually. He communicates to the Hindoos all the progress that thought has made among the Europeans. He is among them, by a much juster title than the Missionaries, the Apostle of Christianity."

Autobiographical Sketch.

THE following letter from RAMMOHUN ROY himself first appeared in the "Athenæum," and in the "Literary Gazette;" from one or other of which it was copied into various newspapers. It was written just before he went to France. It was probably designed for some distinguished person who had desired him to give an outline of his history; and he adopted this form for the purpose. The letter may be considered as addressed to his friend Mr. GORDON, of Calcutta.

"MY DEAR FRIEND,

"In conformity with the wish you have frequently expressed, that I should give you an outline of my life, I have now the pleasure to give you the following very brief sketch.

"My ancestors were Brahmins of a high order, and, from time immemorial, were devoted to the religious duties of their race, down to my fifth progenitor, who about one hundred and forty years ago gave up spiritual exercises for worldly pursuits and aggrandisement. His descendants ever since have followed his example, and, according to the usual fate of courtiers, with various success, sometimes rising to honour and sometimes falling; sometimes rich and sometimes poor; sometimes excelling in success, sometimes miserable through disappointment. But my maternal ancestors, being of the sacerdotal order by profession as well as by birth, and of a family than which none holds a higher rank in that profession, have up to the present day uniformly adhered to a life of religious observances and devotion, preferring peace and tranquillity of mind to the excitements of ambition, and all the allurements of worldly grandeur.

"In conformity with the usage of my paternal race, and the wish of my father, I studied the Persian and Arabic languages,—these being indispensable to those who attached themselves to the courts of the Mahommedan princes; and agreeably to the usage of my maternal relations, I devoted myself to the study of the Sanscrit and the theological works written in it, which contain the body of Hindoo literature, law and religion.

"When about the age of sixteen, I composed a manuscript calling in question the validity of the idolatrous system of the Hindoos. This, together with my known sentiments on that subject, having produced a coolness between me and my immediate kindred, I proceeded on my travels, and passed through different countries, chiefly within, but some beyond, the bounds of Hindoostan, with a feeling of great aversion to the establishment of the British power in India. When I had reached the age of twenty, my father recalled me, and restored me to his favour; after which I first saw and began to associate with Europeans, and soon after made myself tolerably acquainted with their laws and form of Government. Finding them generally more intelligent, more steady and moderate in their conduct, I gave up my prejudice against them, and became inclined in their favour, feeling persuaded that their rule, though a foreign yoke, would lead more speedily and surely to the amelioration of the native inhabitants; and I enjoyed the confidence of several of them even in their public capacity. My continued controversies with the Brahmins on the subject of their idolatry and superstition, and my interference with their custom of burning widows, and other pernicious practices, revived and increased their animosity againat me; and through their influence with my family, my father was again obliged to withdraw his countenance openly. though his limited pecuniary support was still continued to me.

"After my father's death I opposed the advocates of idolatry with still greater boldness. Availing myself of the art of printing now established in India, I published various works and pamphlets against their errors, in the native and foreign languages. This raised such a feeling against me, that I was at last deserted by every person except two or three Scotch friends, to whom, and the nation to which they belong, I always feel grateful.

"The ground which I took in all my controversies was, not that of opposition to Brahminism, but to a perversion of it; and I endeavoured to show that the idolatry of the Brahmins was contrary to the practice of their ancestors, and the principles of the ancient books and authorities, which they profess to revere and obey. Notwithstanding the violence of the opposition and resistance to my opinions, several highly respectable persons both among my own relations and others, began to adopt the same sentiments.

"I now felt a strong wish to visit Europe, and obtain, by personal observation, a more thorough insight into its manners, customs, religion, and political institutions. I refrained, however, from carrying this intention into effect until the friends who coincided in my sentiments should be increased in number and strength. My expectations having been at length realised, in November, 1830, I embarked for England, as the discussion of the

East India Company's charter was expected to come on, by which the treatment of the natives of India, and its future government, would be determined for many years to come, and an appeal to the King in Council, against the abolition of the practice of burning widows, was to be heard before the Privy Council; and his Majesty the Emperor of Delhi had likewise commissioned me to bring before the authorities in England certain encroachments on his rights by the East India Company. I accordingly arrived in England in April, 1831.

"I hope you will excuse the brevity of this sketch, as I have no leisure at present to enter into particulars; and

"I remain, &c.,

"RAMMOHUN ROY."

Miss Mary Carpenter.

U. RAY & SONS.

Chapter 1.

ENGLISH IMPRESSIONS OF RAMMOHUN ROY,

Derived from documents which reached England before his visit.

MORE than half a century has now elapsed since the attention of the religious public in Great Britain was first drawn to the wonderful man who is the subject of the present volume. Those who are acquainted with India at the present time, when the efforts of the British Government have long been directed to advancing the material resources of that great country, as well as to promote intellectual and moral improvement, and who are aware how gladly these efforts are seconded by the intellectual part of the native population can hardly realize the difficulties which the first Hindoo Reformer must have had to encounter. This must be borne in mind when tracing the progress of the extraordinary individual, who, for so long a period, stood alone to encounter the hostility of a whole people sunk in the most degrading idolatry.

The first English notice we find of RAMMOHUN ROY occurs in the Periodical Accounts of the Baptist Missionary Society, Vol. VI., pp. 106—109, of the date of 1816—

"RAMA-MOHUNA-RAYA, a very rich Rarhee Brahmun of Calcutta, is a respectable Sungskrita scholar, and so well versed in Persian, that he is called MOULUVEE-RAMA-MOHUNA-RAYA* ; he also writes English with correctness, and reads with ease English mathematical and metaphysical works. He has published in Bengalee one or two philosophical works, form the Sungskrita, which he hopes may be useful in leading his countrymen to renounce idolatry. Europeans breakfast at his house, at a separate table, in the English fashion ; he has paid us a visit at Serampore, and at a late interview, after relating an anecdote of Krishna, relative to a petty theft by this god, he added, "The sweeper of my house would not do such an act, and can I worship a god sunk lower than the man who is a menial servant ? He is at present a simple theist, admires Jesus Christ, but knows not his *need* of the atonement. He has not renoun-

* In this and other extracts the original orthography is preserved.

ced his caste, and this enables him to visit the richest families of Hindoos. He is said to be very moral; but is pronounced to be a most wicked man by the strict Hindoos."

Subjoined to this is a copy of RAMMOHUN ROY'S Preface to his Translation of the Abridgment of the Vedanta. The passage closes as follows:

"Of this man Mr. YATES writes thus, in a letter dated Aug. 1816:—'I was introduced to him about a year ago: before this, he was not acquainted with any one who cared for his soul. Some time after, I introduced EUSTACE CAREY to him, and we have had repeated conversation with him. When I first knew him he would talk only on metaphysical subjects, such as the eternity of matter, the nature and qualities of evidence, &c., but he has lately become much more humble, and disposed to converse about the gospel. He has many relations, Brahmuns, and has established religious worship among them. He maintains the unity of God, and hates all the heathen idolatries. He visited EUSTACE lately and stayed to family prayer, with which he was quite delighted. EUSTACE gave him Dr. WATT'S Hymns; he said he would treasure them up in his heart. He has been at Serampore once, and has engaged to come and see me in the course of a few weeks. He has offered EUSTACE a piece of ground for a school."

A fuller account of RAMMOHUN ROY is found in the Church of England "Missionary Register" for Sept., 1816, p. 370 :—

"We have been favoured with a sight of a tract, printed at Calcutta in the present year (1816), with the following title :—'Translation of an Abridgment of the Vedant, or Resolution of all the Veds; the most celebrated and revered Work of Brahminical Theology, establishing the Unity of the Supreme Being; and that he alone is the Object of propitiation and worship. By RAMMOHUN ROY.' Before we give an account of this curious tract, it may be advantageous to our readers to know something of the author. Of RAMMOHUN ROY we have received reports from several friends. The substance of them is this: he is a Brahmin, about 32 years of age, of extensive landed property, and of great consideration and influence; shrewd, vigilant, active, ambitious, prepossessing in his manners, versed in various languages, and busily employed in giving lectures to a number of his countrymen on the Unity of the Godhead. He is acquainted with the New Testament, and seems disposed to hear any thing which can be enforced by the authority of Christ.

"Another account carries him further as a Christian. It states that he began his studies by learning Persian ; as he considered a knowledge of that language necessary to every native of any distinction. From Persian he was led almost as a matter of course to Arabic and the Koran. His own statement is, that the religion of Mahomed at first made some impression upon him ; but when he found that the prophet carried off the beautiful wife of his slave, and attempted to establish his religion by the sword, he became convinced that it could not be from God. Then he studied our Bible in English ; and in consequence became a Christian. He has spread his doctrine to a considerable extent and has several Hindoos of high caste and of fortune in league with him, who maintain his opinions. They call themselves a society, and are bound by certain rules, one of which is, that no man shall be admitted into their number except with this condition, that he renounce idol worship. Of these rules however, they do not seem to be very uniform in the observance. One of the society, though he professess to have renounced idolatry, yet keeps in his house a number of gods, as well as two large pagodas ; his society granted him a dispensation on this head, because he possesses a certain quantity of land from the King of Delhi for this purpose, and if he were to destroy his idols, he might lose his land. One account carries the number of RAMMOHUN'S followers to nearly five hundred; and states, that they expect soon to be strong enough to enable him publicly to avow his faith, and consequently to lose his caste, which he has hitherto not done, as it would impede his intercourse with many whom he hopes shortly to convince. The Brahmins had twice attempted his life, but he was fully on his guard. It is stated, that after being baptized he intends to embark for England, with many of his friends, in order to pass some years in the acquisition of learning at one or both of our universities.

"RAMMOHUN writes and speaks English correctly. He has published different tracts and translations in our tongue, and in Persian and Bengalee, directed against the Hindoo idolatry and superstitions. The piece, of which we shall give an abstract, discovers little else than a discernment of the folly of the vulgar belief of his country; and a subtle, but unsuccessful, attempt to put a good meaning on the absurd statements of its more ancient and refined creed. His judgment may possibly be convinced of the truth of Divine revelation, but one of our correspondents represents him to be as yet but a selfconfident Deist;—disgusted with the follies of the pretended revelations from heaven, with which he has been conversant, but not yet bowed in his convictions, and humbled in his heart to the revelation of Divine mercy. We do not mean to say that the heart of RAMMOHUN ROY is not humbled, and that he has not received the gospel as the only remedy for the spiritual diseases under which he labours in common with all men ; but we have as yet seen no evidence sufficient to warrant us in this belief. We pray God to give him grace, that he may in penitence and faith embrace with all his heart the Saviour of the world.

The tract (of which we have given the title) is short, extending to fourteen pages, quarto. It is an abridgment of the Vedant of VYAS, whom RAMMOHUN ROY represents as 'the greatest of the Indian theologists, philosophers and poets. The author professes to give the real sense and meaning of the Vedant and Veds on the most important points of the Hindoo theology, which he asserts to have been misunderstood and forgotten. His various positions are supported by passages from the Vedant or Veds, and those which appear to contradict them are explained. After asserting the necessity for mankind to acquire knowledge respecting the Supreme Being, but that this knowledge is limited to very narrow bounds, the author argues from the Vedant and

Veds that creating and governing power cannot be attributed to any of the various objects to which the grosser Hindoo theology attributes it; such as the void space, air, light, nature, atoms, the soul, any god or goddess of the earth, the sun, or any of the celestial gods. He asserts the unity, spirituality, omnipresence and omnipotence of the Supreme Being;—that he is the sole object of worship;—that the adoration of him is required of mankind, as well as of the celestial gods;—that moral principle is a part of the adoration of God, with reliance on, and self-resignation to, the only true Being, and an aversion to worldly considerations,—and that devotion to the Supreme Being is not limited to any holy place or sacred country.

"The rise of this new sect, the zeal and subtlety displayed by its founder, with its obvious tendency to undermine the fabric of Hindoo superstition, are objects of serious attention to the Christian mind. Who knows, asks one of the friends form whom we have received these communications but this man may be one of the many instruments by which God, in his mysterious providence, may accomplish the overthrow of idolatry?' 'What may be the effect of this man's labours,' says another correspondent, 'time will shew.' Probably, they may bring the craft of Brahminism and caste into danger; and God may be in this manner shaking the kingdom of Satan. However, this may prove, that great work will be done; and though reason and philosophy may not have a voice powerful enough to reach the hearts of these poor captives, yet the Christian missionary whom Christ sends forth will find a mouth and tongue which no man shall be able to gainsay or to resist'." *

In this, and in other extracts, the Editor of this volume refrains from expressing an opinion on the sentiments of the writer, and merely presents to the reader the views which were entertained at the time respecting RAMMOHUN ROY, and brought before the English public by the periodical literature of the day.

A notice of the Abridgment of the Vedant occurs in the same volume of the "Monthly Repository," p. 512, which is interesting, as affording from another quarter a view of the position first taken by Hindoo Reformer:—

"Two literary phenomena, of a singular nature, have very recenty been exhibited in India. The first is a Hindu Deist.

"RAMMOHUN ROY, a Brahmin, has published a

* Extracted from the "Monthly Repository of Theology and General Literature," Vol XIII., pp. 299—301, 1818.

small work, in the present year, at Calcutta, entitled 'An Abridgment of the Vedant, or Resolution of all the Veds ; the most celebrated work of Brahminical Theology, establishing the Unity of the Supreme Being, and that he alone is the Object of Worship.' It contains a collection of very remarkable texts from the Vedas, in which the principles of natural religion are delivered, not without dignity ; and which treat all worship to inferior beings, together with the observance of rites and seasons, and the distinctions of food, as the aids of an imperfect religion, which may be altogether disregarded by those who have attained to the knowledge and love of the true God. His contemporaries and his ancestors he considers as idolaters, notwithstanding the excuse of an allegorical theology which some Europeans have made for them. This Brahmin is made to complain with feeling in the English version, of the obloquy which he has incurred among his countrymen by the purity of his faith. He alludes no where to any other system of religion ; and passes over, in absolute silence, the labours, and indeed the existence of the missionaries."

The records of the next year mark a striking advance in RAMMOHUN ROY'S mind. The following passage is extracted from a letter from Rev. T. BELSHAM, Minister of Essex Street Chapel,

London, as an introduction to a letter he had just received from a native convert to Christianity, WILLIAM ROBERTS, of Madras:—

"It is very remarkable that while the great doctrine of the unity and unrivalled supremacy of God is thus gradually working its way among the poorer classes of natives in the vicinity of Madras, it is at the same time making a triumphant progress among the higher castes of Hidoos in the great and populous city of Calcutta. RAMMOHUN ROY, a learned, eloquent, and opulent Brahmin, having, by the proper exercise of his own understanding, discovered the folly and absurdity of the Hindoo mythology and of idol worship, was led by a conscientious sense of duty to proclaim this important discovery to his countrymen, and has publicly taught the doctrine of the divine unity and perfection to the native Hindoos, and has entered his protest against their impious, barbarous and idolatrous rites. Such doctrine from a person of such exalted rank, at first excited great astonishment, and gave infinite offence. But by degrees the courage, eloquence, and perseverance of this extraordinary man prevailed over all opposition: and it is said that many hundreds of the native Hindoos, and especially of the young people, have embraced his doctrine. He does not profess to be a Christiain. He told a worthy clergyman at

Calcutta about a year ago, that he preferred Christianity to all other religions, and would certainly embrace it, if it were not for the doctrine of the Trinity. This was an insurmountable obstacle. At the beginning of this year, in January, 1817, he informed the same respectable clergyman, that he was now in the way of ascertaining whether the doctrine of the Trinity is or is not the doctrine of the New Testament: for that he and twenty other learned Brahmins had determined to sit down and study the Gospel with the greatest possible attention and impartiality, in order to discover their real meaning; and he did not think it possible that twenty serious and impartial inquirers, who sought after nothing but truth, and who earnestly implored divine illumination and direction, would be suffered to fall into an erroneous conclusion. The result of this inquiry has not yet reached England." *

During the years 1816, 1817, RAMMOHUN ROY issued various pamphlets, of which a list is given in the Appendix, all tending to prove to his countrymen the unity of the deity from their own sacred writings. These were translated into English, and a full review of them is given in the "Monthly Repository" for 1819, Vol. XIV., pp.

* "Christian Reformer," Vol. IV., p. 2, 1818.

561—569. As these works are probably inaccessible to most readers, some extracts from this review will be interesting as indicating the modes of thought of the author :—

"The 'Ishopanished' is another chapter of the Veds, strongly asserting, as the pious translator says, 'that the sole regulator of the universe is but one, omnipresent, surpassing our powers of comprehension, above external sense, whose worship is the chief duty of mankind, and the sole cause of eternal beatitude.' In the Preface is obviated the objection that the *Puranas*, &c., admitted expositions of the Hindoo shasters or sacred books, inculcate 'the worship of the several gods and goddesses.' 'They affrm frequently,' says the Reformer, 'that the directions to worship any figured beings are only applicable to those who are incapable of elevating their minds to the idea of an invisible Supreme Being, in order that such persons, by fixing their attention on those invented figures, may be able to restrain themselves from vicious temptations, and that those that are competent for the worship of the invisible God should disregard the worship of idols.'

"Many learned Brahmins are perfectly aware of the absurdity of idolatry, and are well informed of the nature of the purer mode of divine worship, But as in the rites, ceremonies and festivals of idolatry, they find the source of their comforts and fortune, they not only never fail to protect idol worship from all attacks, but even advance and encourage it to the utmost of their power, by keeping the knowledge of their Scriptures concealed from the rest of the people. Their followers, too, confiding in these leaders, feel gratification in the idea of the Divine nature residing in a being resembilng themselves in birth, shape, and propensities ; and are naturally delighted with a mode of worship agreeable to the senses, though destructive of moral principles, and the fruitful parent of prejudice and superstition.'—*Pref.*, pp. ix. x.

"The zealous writer goes on to controvert the liberal opinion of some Europeans that the Hindoos regard their idols, as the Roman Catholics say they do their crucifixes and pictures, as mere helps to contemplation ; an opinion, he says, which very naturally arises out of 'the extreme absurdity of pure, unqualified idolatry,' and under which, 'flimsy and borrowed' as it is, he is glad to see the Hindoos willing to shelter their practices, in as much as such a disposition shews that they are beginning to be sensible of their folly. He declares, however, that 'Hindoos of the present age with a very few exceptions,' are downright and gross idolaters.

"For whatever Hindoo purchases an idol in

the market, or constructs one with his own hands, or has one made up under his own superintendence, it is his invariable practice to perform certain ceremonies, called *Pran Pratishtha* or the endowment of animation, by which he believes that its nature is changed from that of the mere materials of which it is formed, and that it acquires not only life but supernatural powers. Shortly afterwards, if the idol be of the masculine gender, he marries it to a feminine one, with no less pomp and magnificence than he celebrates the nuptials of his own children. The mysterious process is now complete, and the god and goddess are esteemed the arbiters of his destiny, and continually receive his most ardent adoration.

" 'At the same time, the worshipper of images ascribes to them at once the opposite natures of human and of superhuman beings. In attention to their supposed wants as living beings, he is seen feeding, or pretending to feed them, every morning and evening; and as in the hot season he is careful to fan them, so in the cold he is equally regardful of their comfort, covering them by day and night with warm clothing, and placing them at night in a snug bed.'—*Pref*, pp. xiii xiv.

"The doctrine of the Vedant that, 'God is everywhere and every thing is in God,' which is, it seems, pleaded in behalf of Hindoo idolatry, amounts to no more, according to RAMMOHUN ROY, than 'that nothing is absent from God, and nothing bears real existence except by the volition of God, whose existence is the sole support of the conceived existence of the universe, which is acted upon by him in the same manner as a human body is by a soul.'

"Reformers are opposed everywhere by the same prejudices. Idolatry is defended in Hindoostan by the argument of custom.

"'Let the authors of the Veds, Poorans and Tantras,' it is said, 'assert what they may in favour of devotion to the Supreme Being, but idol worship has been practised for so many centuries that custom renders it proper to continue that worship.' It is, however, evident to every one possessed of common sense, that custom or fashion is quite different from divine faith; the latter proceeding from spiritual authorities and correct reasoning and the former being merely the fruit of vulgar caprice. What can justify a man, who believes in the inspiration of his religious books, in neglecting the direct authorities of the same works, and subjecting himself entirely to custom and fashion, which are liable to perpetual changes, and depend upon popular whim?

" 'I may conclude this subject with an appeal to the good sense of my countrymen by asking them whose advice appears the most disinterested and most rational,—that of those who, concealing your Scriptures from you, continually teach you thus: "believe whatever we may say—don't examine or even touch your Scriptures—neglect entirely your reasoning faculties—do not only consider us, whatever may be our principles, as gods on earth, but humbly adore and propitiate us by sacrificing to us the greater part (if not the whole) of your property;" or that of the man who lays your Scriptures and their comments, as well as their translations, before you, and solicits you to examine their purport, without neglecting the proper and moderate use of reason; and to attend strictly to their directions, by the rational performance of your duty to your sole Creator, and to your fellow-creatures, and also to pay true respect to those who think and act righteously? I hope no one can be so prejudiced as to be unable to discern which advice is most calculated to lead him to the best road to both temporal and eternal happiness'— pp xxi—XXIII.

"After the Preface is an introduction, which we lay before the reader as a whole, on account of the pure moral feeling which it expresses:

"The physical powers of man are limited; and when viewed comparatively, sink into insignificance; while in the same ratio his moral faculties rise in our estimation, as embracing a wide sphere of action, and possessing a capability of almost boundless improvement. If the short duration of human life be contrasted with the great age of the universe, and the limited extent of bodily strength with the many objects to which there is a necessity of applying it, we must necessarily be disposed to entertain but a very humble opinion of our own nature; and nothing, perhaps, is so well calculated to restore our self-complacency as the contemplation of our more extensive moral powers, together with the highly beneficial objects which the appropriate exercise of them may produce. On the other hand, sorrow and remorse can scarcely fail, sooner or later, to be the portion of him who is conscious of having neglected opportunities of rendering benefit to his fellow-creatures. From considerations like these, it has been that I (although born a *Brahmin*, and instructed in my youth in all the principles of that sect), being thoroughly convinced of the lamentable errors of my countrymen, have been stimulated to employ every means in my power to improve their minds, and lead them to the knowledge of a purer system of morality. Living constantly among *Hindoos* of different sects and professions, I have had ample opportunity of observing the superstitious puerilities into which they have been thrown by their self-interested guides; who, in defiance of the law as well as of common sense, have succeeded but too well in conducting them to the temple of idolatry; and while they hid from their view the true substance of morality, have infused into their simple hearts a weak attachment for its mere shadow. For the chief part of the theory and practice of *Hindooism*, I am sorry to say, is made to consist in the adoption of a peculiar mode of diet, the least aberration from which (even though the conduct of the offender may in other respects be pure and blameless) is not only visited with the severest censure, but actually punished by exclusion from the society of his family and friends. In a word, he is doomed to undergo what is commonly called loss of caste. On the contrary, the rigid observance of this grand article of *Hindoo* faith, is considered in so high a light as to compensate for every moral defect. Even the most atrocious crimes weigh little or nothing in the balance against the supposed guilt of its violation. Murder, theft, or perjury though brought home to the party by a judicial sentence, so far from inducing loss or caste, is visited in their society with no peculiar mark of infamy or disgrace. A trifling present to the *Brahmin*, commonly called *Prayaschit*, with the performance of a few idle ceremonies, are held as a sufficient atonement for all those crimes ; and the delinquent is at once freed from all temporal inconvenience, as well as all dread of future retribution. My reflections upon these solemn truths have been most painful for many years. I have never ceased to contemplate, with the strongest feelings of regret, the obstinate adherence of my countrymen to their fatal system of idolatry, inducing for the sake of propitiating their supposed deities, the violation of every humane and social feeling. And this in various instances, but more especially in the dreadful acts of self-destruction, and the immolation of the nearest relations, under the delusion of conforming to sacred religious rites. I have never ceased, I repeat, to contemplate these practices with the strongest feelings of regret, and to view in then the moral debasement of a race who, I cannot help thinking, are capable of better things ; whose susceptibility, patience and mildness of character, render them worthy of a better destiny. Under these impressions, therefore, I have been compelled to lay before them genuine translations of parts of their Scripture, which inculcates not only the enlightened worship of one God, but the purest principles of morality, accompanied with such notices as I deemed requisite to oppose the arguments employed by the *Brahmins* in defence of their beloved system. Most earnestly do I pray that the whole may, sooner or later, prove efficient in producing on the minds of *Hindoos* in general, a conviction of the rationality of believing in and adoring the Supreme Being only ; together with a complete perception, and practice of that grand and comprehensive moral principle, 'Do unto others as ye would be done by.' "

This courageous attack on the long-established and prevailing religion of his countrymen is most remarkable, when we consider that the author of it was brought up in the midst of gross idolatry, and with none around him to guide him to a purer religion, or to open his eyes to its baneful nature, in perverting the moral nature of man, and degrading the whole system of society. Such an instance is probably unparalleled in the history of the world. The Hindoo Reformer had entered on a mighty conflict, single handed. RAMMOHUN ROY was speedily attacked in his own language by an "Apologist for the present system of Hindoo worship," and by an "Advocate for Idolatry, at Madras," who published a letter against him in the *Madras Courier*. Notwithstanding all opposition, however, he succeeded in awaking the attention of many of his countrymen, by the simple force of truth, set forth by his masterly mind. When writing to the Editor of the Translation of the Cena Upanishad, he says at the close of a letter from which extracts were made in the Biographical Sketch:—

"I now with the greatest pleasure inform you, that several of my countrymen have risen superior to their prejudices; many are inclined to seek for the truth; and a great number of those who dissented form me have now coincided with me in opinion. The engagement has prevented my proceeding to Europe as soon as I could wish; but you may depend upon my setting off for England within a short period of time, and if you do not return to India before October next, you will most probably receive a letter from me informing you of the exact time of my departure for England, and of the name of the vessel on which I shall embark."

The European reputation of RAMMOHUN ROY as a remarkable man, and a Reformer, was not confined to Great Britain. A French pamphlet respecting him was forwarded to the Editor of the "Monthly Repository," (xv, 1820,) by the Abbé GREGOIRE, formerly Bishop of Blois, and which was afterwards inserted in the "Chronique

Religieuse" The biographical part of this pamphlet was derived from cmmunications from the learned M. D' ACOSTA, then the Editor of *The Times*, at Calcutta. The following extract presents several interesting features of the life of RAMMOHUN ROY, as viewed by a foreigner :—

"Whatever be the abstract merit of RAMMOHUN ROY, there is, probably, throughout India no Brahmin who is less a Hindoo than he ; and thousands of dupes who have suffered the loss of their caste have been less offenders against the peculiarities of their religion than he.

"RAMMOHUN ROY, considering that youth is the period most adapted to the reception of novelties, either good or bad, has established a school at his own expense, where fifty children are taught Sanscrit, English, and Geography. How slender soever these attempts at reform may appear, they will, probably more or less rapidly attain their object ; aided as they are by European influence, and, above all, by the art of printing. It is against the division of his countrymen into castes that RAMMOHUN ROY'S correcting hand is turned, and in that the strength of his judgment is evinced. The distinction of castes may be regarded as the cement of the polytheism and the other errors prevalent in India : let that distinction disappear, and all the Hindoo superstitions will crumble beneath the touch of human reason. It is the division into castes, carried to a frightful excess, which consolidates the Hindoo system, by incorporating it with the daily habits of domestic life. In fact, European institutions themselves are not altogether exempt from the influence of this vicious principle : legitimacy, taken as an absolute rule ; hereditary nobility and the privileges of the first-born, are the same thing ; or rather, are remnants of it, which cannot without difficulty be destroyed.

"RAMMOHUN ROY, adapting his measures to the place and the times in which he lives, as well as the sort of men he is attempting to enlighten, does not oppose the institution of castes by abstract reasonings (for they would be useless), but by the authority of the Vedant, which he is careful not to bring into disrepute, and of which he professes to be but the commentator. The discretion which regulates his conduct prevents any action revolting to the prejudices of his fellow-sectaries, or capable of affording an excuse for his exclusion. He has, nevertheless, risen above many littlenesses : he scruples not to seat himself with an European who is eating ; sometimes he even invites Europeans to his house, and treats them according to their own taste. Far, however, from wishing to lose his Brahminical dignity, it is upon *that* he founds his enterprise ; asserting that it is his duty, as a Brahmin, to instruct his countrymen in the sense and in the real commands of their sacred books. His efforts are directed towards the destruction of that prejudice which prevents the different castes from eating together. He considers that this amelioration is the most essential, and will affect every other, even the *political*, amelioration of his country—and this is an object to which he is not indifferent. Every six months he publishes a little tract, in Bengalee and in English, developing his system of theism; and he is always ready to answer the pamphlets published at Calcutta or Madras in opposition to him. He takes pleasure in this controversy; but although far from deficient in philosophy, or in knowledge, he distinguishes himself more by his logical mode of reasoning than by his general views. He appears to feel the advantage which it gives him with the Methodists, some of whom are endeavouring to convert him. He seems to have prepared himself for his polemical career from the logic of the Arabians, which he regards as superior to every other; he asserts, likewise, that he has found nothing in European books equal to the scholastic philosophy of the Hindoos.

"We may easily imagine that a man who has raised himself so much above the level of his countrymen by his intellectual attainments, cannot exactly resemble them in his conduct. He not only refrains from their superstitious practices (which is not saying much in his favour, since he might do so from various causes not highly laudable), but, what is much more important, all his conversation, his actions and manners,e vince a powerful sentiment of individual dignity; whilst, in general, meanness and feebleness of mind are characteristic of the Hindoo. Influenced, like those around him, with the spirit of order, economy and knowledge of the value of money, acquired by their mercantile education. RAMMOHUN ROY does n t view the augmentation of property as the most important object: his fortune consists of the wealth he received form his ancestors: he does not give his mind to any kind of commercial speculation. He would consider that mode of life beneath his station and the duties of a Brahmin. He derives no pecuniary advantage from his works; and, in all probability, desirous as he may be of power and distinction, he would not accept of the Government any place that should be merely lucrative; to *solicit* one, of any description he would not condescend. It is not likely, however, that the Government will make trial of his inclination; it would not suit the policy of the present masters of his country to give encouragement to a subject whose soul is so lofty, and whose ingenuous conversation often shews, in a strain half serious and half jesting, all that he wishes to be able to do for his country. He cultivates a friendly connexion with many Europeans, distinguished by their rank or their merit ; he appears not to seek connexions of any other kind. Within the last year or two he has been less in society than formerly.

"RAMMOHUN ROY, as has already been shewn, is not yet forty years old ; he is tall and robust ; his regular features and habitually grave countenance assume a most pleasing appearance when he is animated. He appears to have a slight disposition to melancholy. The whole of his conversation and manners shew, at first sight, that he is above mediocrity. He frequently talks of going into Europe, but apparently considers it desirable first to molify so far the prejudices of his countrymen that he may not by that voyage, which is regarded as unlawful, expose himself to excommunication. It is very doubtful whether he will succeed in this attempt ; the hope, however, which he cherishes, is a decided proof of the character of his mind. * * *

"It is singular that this philosophic Indian, who, as has been shewn in this little sketch, has enlarged views respecting the amelioration of the men of his country, has not the least idea of improving the females, of whom he avoids even the mention. We must suppose that this sort of prejudice, inspired by the Shasters, though general amongst the Hindoos, has been perpetuated in so enlightened a mind only by the circumstances of RAMMOHUN ROY's domestic life: it is known that every member of his family verifies the proverb, by opposing with the greatest vehemence all his projects of reform. None of them, not even his wife, would accompany him to Calcutta; in consequence of which he rarely visits them in Bordouan, where they reside. They have disputed with him even the superintendence of the education of his nephews; and his fanatical mother shews as much ardour in her incessant opposition to him, as he displays in his attempts to destroy the idolatry of the Hindoos.

"CALCUTTA, *Nov.* 8, 1818."*

A testimony from a different source is not less interesting; it has been already alluded to in the Biographical Sketch. It is taken from p. 106 of a "Journal of a Route across India, through Egypt to England, in the years 1817 and 1818. By Lieut.—Col. FITZCLARENCE" 4to. 1819:—

* "Monthly Repository," Vol. xv. pp. 2—4.

"There has never been, to my knowledge, an instance of any Hindoo of condition or caste being converted to our faith. The only conversion of any kind, if it can be called so, that has come within my observation was that of a high-caste Brahmin, of one of the first families in the country, who is not only perfect master of the Sanscrit, but has gained a thorough acquaintance with the English language and literature, and has openly declared that the Brahminical religion is in its purity a pure Deism, and not the gross polytheism into which it has degenerated. I became well acquainted with him, and admire his talents and acquirements. His eloquence in our language is very great, and I am told he is still more admirable in Arabic and Persian. It is remarkable, that he has studied and thoroughly understands the politics of Europe, but more particularly those of England; and the last time I was in his company he argued forcibly against a standing army in a free country, and quoted all the arguments brought forward by the Members of the Opposition. I think that he is in many respects a most extraordinary person. In the first place, he is a religious reformer, who has, amongst a people more bigoted than those of Europe in the middle ages, dared to think for himself. His learning is most extensive, as he is not only conversant with the best books in English, Arabic, Sanscrit, Bengalee and Hindoostanee, but has even studied rhetoric in Arabic and English and quotes LOCKE and BACON on all occasions. From the view he thus takes of the religion, manners and customs of so many nations, and from his having observed the number of different modes of addressing and worshipping the Supreme Being, he naturally turned to his own faith with an unprejudiced mind, found it perverted with the religion of the Vedas to a gross idolatry, and was not afraid, though aware of the consequences to publish to the world in Bengalee and English his feelings and opinions on the subject; of course he was fully prepared to meet the host of interested enemies who from sordid motives, wished to keep the lower classes in a state of the darkest ignorance. I have understood that his family have quitted him—that he has been declared to have lost caste—and is for the present, as all religious reformers must be for a time, a mark to be scoffed at. To a man of his sentiments and rank this loss of caste must be particularly painful, but at Calcutta he associates with the English: he is, however, cut off from all familiar and domestic intercourse; indeed, from all communication of any kind with his relations and former friends. His name is RAMMOHUN ROY. He is particularly handsome, not of a very dark complexion, of a fine person, and most courtly manners. He professes to have no objection to eat and live as we do, but refrains from it, in order not to expose himself to the imputation of having changed his religion for the good things of this world. He will sit at table with us while the meat is on it, which no other Brahmin will do. He continues his native dress, but keeps a carriage, being a man of some property. He is very desirous to visit England and enter one of our universities where I shall be most anxious to see him, and to learn his ideas of our country, its manners and customs."

We have already seen, in the introductory Biographical Sketch how gradually the mind of the great Hindoo Reformer became attracted to Christianity ; how he devoted some of the most important years of his life to the study of Hebrew and Greek, that he may himself judge of the real meaning of the Christian Scriptures ; and how, being eventually fully satisfied that they taught nothing inconsistent with pure monotheism, he presented to his countrymen, as their "guide to peace and happiness," his "Precepts of Jesus."

* "Monthly Repository," Vol. xv. p. 7.

To this he refers in the following extract from a letter dated Calcutta, Sept. 5, 1820:—

"As to the opinion intimated by Sir SAMUEL T——R, respecting the medium course in Christian dogmas, I never have attempted to oppose it. I regret only that the followers of Jesus, in general, should have paid much greater attention to inquiries after his nature than to the observance of his commandments, when we are well aware that no human acquirements can ever discover the nature even of the most common and visible things, and, moreover, that such inquiries are not enjoined by the divine revelation·

"On this consideration I have compiled serveral passages of the New Tesatment which I thought essensial to Christianity, and published them under the designation of Precepts of Jesus, at which the Missionaries at Shrainampoor have expressed great displeasure, and called me, in their review of the tract, an injurer of the cause of truth. I was, therefore, under the necessity of defending myself in an 'Appeal to the Christian Public,' a few copies of which tracts I have the preasure to send you, under the care of Captain S——and intreat your acceptance of them."

The writings of RAMMOHUN ROY and the controversy which they excited attiacted so much notice in British India, that an atricle appeared on the subject in the "Asiatic Department of the *Calcutta Journal* of Politics and General Literature," No. VIII., for Aug. 1821. Long and very interesting extracts are made from this and other Indian papers in the "Monthly Repository" for 1822, Vol. XVII. pp. 393—400. Though the whole of this might be very important and interesting in an extended memoir, yet space prevents our doing more than copy the following letter, which occurs in the *Journal* of August 1, 1821, pp. 405, 406:—

"*To the Editor of the Calcutta Journal.*

"SIR,—RAM MOHUN ROY may be known by name to most of your readers, and it is probable, that many of them have heard he has forsaken the idolatry and all the superstitions of the Hindoos; but excepting those who are personally acquainted with, him, few are likely to be duly informed of his acquirements, his conduct, and his present religious belief. The Second Appeal to the Christian Public in defence of the 'Precepts of Jesus,' a work lately published by him, will make us acquainted with his religious belief, will enable us to form some idea of his acquirements, and cannot fail of producing in every *Christian*, great regard for the author, and a strong interest concerning so illustrious an individual; and the more we learn of his conduct the more will he be raised in our estimation.

"The worthy motives by which RAMMOHUN ROY is actuated, have caused him to print the work in question, and several previous works, at his own expense, to distribute them among his acquaintance and such other persons as are likely to take an interest in the important subjects on which he has written. His last publication, that above-mentioned, is too large to be reprinted in a newspaper; but its contents are so important, and do the author so much credit, that I hope some competent person will prepare a compendium therof, and have the same published in the *Calcutta Journal.* In the mean time, you will oblige me by printing the two portions which accompany this letter: the first portion commences in p. 159, and ends in p 164; the other commences in p. 172, and extends to the end of the work. If such persons as on reading these extracts feel a sufficient interest to desire to peruse the work with attention, apply to the author for copies, it is probable he will readily comply with their request, as far as the number of copies printed will admit.

"Here we observe an individual, born and bred in a country benighted under the most gross idolatry and superstition, who, by a just use of that understanding which our gracious Creator has given to mankind to guide them to all truths, having discovered the falsehood of that system of idolatry and the absurdity of those superstitions, conscientiously abandoned both, and thereby subjected himself to inconveniences and dangers of which persons living in more enlightened societies can hardly form an idea. Next, he directed his attention to the Christian religion; and that same just and honest use of his understanding, which discovered the falsehood and absurdity of idolatry and superstition, satisfied him that *Jesus* was the Messiah, that he was employed by God to reveal his will to men, and to make known to them the only true religion. He observed the internal and historical evidence of Christanity to be such as demonstrated its truth. Blessed with the light of Christianity, he dedicates his time and his money not only to release his countrymen from the state of degradation in which they exist, but also to diffuse among the European masters of his country, the sole true religion—as it was promulgated by Christ, his apostles and his disciples.

"A FIRM BELIEVER IN CHRIST.

"CALCUTTA, *July* 12, 1821."

The Hindoo Reformer having fully satisfied himself of the importance of the Christian Religion, devoted himself earnestly to support it, and entered into communication on the subject not only with England but with the United States. In a letter addressed by him to a gentleman of Baltimore dated Calcutta, October 27, 1822, he says (*vide* "Monthly Repository" for 1825, Vol. XVIII., p. 433) :—

"I have now every reason to hope, that the truths of Christianity will not be much longer kept hidden under the veil of heathen doctrines and practices, gradually introduced among the followers of Christ, since many lovers of truth are zealously engaged in rendering the religion of Jesus clear from corruptions. * * * I rely much on the force of truth, which will, I am sure, ultimately prevail. Our number is comparatively small, but I am glad to inform you, that none of them can be justly charged with the want of zeal and prudence.

"I wish to add, in order that you may set me right, if you find me mistaken,—my view of Christianity is, that in representing all mankind as the children of one eternal father, it enjoins them to love one another, without making any distinction of country, caste, colour, or creed ; notwithstanding, they may be justified in the sight of the Creator in manifesting their respect towards each other, according to the propriety of their actions, and the reasonableness of their religious opinions and observance.

"I shall loose no time in sending you my Final Appeal to the Christian Public, as soon as it is printed."

In a second letter (Dec. 9, 182) RAMMOHUN ROY remarks :—

"Although our adversaries are both numerous and zealous, as the adversaries of truth always have been, yet our prospects are by no means discouraging, if we only have the means of following up what has already been done.

"We confidently hope that, through these various means, the period will be accelerated, when the belief in the Divine Unity, and in the mission of Christ, will universally prevail,"

We have already seen, in the Biographical Sketch, that RAMMOHUN ROY was not allowed to print his "Final Appeal" at the Baptist Missionary Press, and to give it to the public, at his own expense he set up a Unitarian Press at Dhurmtollah.* It was subsequently published in London by the Unitarian Society in a large octavo volume, together with the "First and Second Appeal," the "Precepts of Jesus," and the prefaces of the author. The final paragraphs of the work are highly characteristic :—

"I tender my humble thanks for the Editor's

* An original copy of the first work issued from it is in the possession of the Editor of this work, having been sent by the noble author to her father, the late Rev. Dr. CARPENTER.

kind suggestion, in inviting me to adopt the doctrine of the Holy Trinity; but I am sorry to find that I am unable to benefit by his advice. After I have long relinquished every idea of a plurality of Gods, or of the persons of the Godhead, taught under different systems of modern Hindooism, I cannot conscientiously and consistently embrace one of a similar nature, though greatly refined by the religious reformations of modern times; since whatever arguments can be adduced against a plurality of Gods strike with equal force against the doctrine of a plurality of persons of the Godhead; and, on the other hand, whatever excuse may be pleaded in favour of a plurality of persons of the Deity, can be offered with equal propriety in defence of polytheism.

"I now conclude my essay by offering up thanks to the Supreme Disposer of the events of this universe for having unexpectedly delivered this country from the long-continued tyranny of its former rulers, and placed it under the government of the English, a nation who not only are blessed with the enjoyment of civil and political liberty, but also interest themselves in promoting liberty and social happiness, as well as free inquiry into literary and religious subjects, among those nations to which their influence extends." *

* "Monthly Repository," 1823, vol. XVIII. p. 479.

The satisfaction which RAMMOHUN ROY received form the mark of appreciation shown him by the publication of his work in England, is shown by the following extract from a letter from him to Dr. T. REES, of London (*vide* "Monthly Repository," 1824, Vol. XIX., pp. 681, 682):—

"REVEREND SIR,—I received your letter of the 16th June last, accompanied by a parcel of books to my address, with feelings of peculiar gratification. I cannot but be proud of the honour which the Committee have conferred upon me in reprinting my compilation of 'The Precepts of Jesus,' and the two Appeals in its defence. I beg you will oblige me by communicating to the members my warm acknowledgments for so distinguished a mark of their approbation. I also beg you will accept my best thanks for your valuable present of the Racovian Catechism, which I shall not fail to read with due attention.

"I have no language to express the happiness I derive form the idea that so many friends of truth, both in England and America, are engaged in attempting to free the originally pure, simple and practical religion of Christ from the heathenish doctrines and absurd notions gradually introduced under the Roman power;

and I sincerely pray that the success of those gentlemen may be as great as (if not greater than) that of LUTHER and others, to whom the religious world is indebted for laying the first stone of religious reformation, and having recommended the system of distinguishing divine authority from human creeds, and the practice of benevolence from ridiculous outward observances."

The effect of his zealous devotion to the cause of truth on his worldly position, both with his countrymen and English residents, may be easily imagined. He bore it all nobly and unflinchingly. The following testimony to him on this point is valuable. It is from Mr. J. S. BUCKINGHAM, who, from his arrival in India, in june, 1818, had ample opportunities of knowing him. It is from a letter dated 68 Baker Street, Portman Square, London, Aug. 4, 1823:—

"RAMMOHUN ROY might have had abundant opportunities of receiving rewards from the Indian Government, in the shape of offices and appointments, for his mere neutrality; but being as remarkable for his integrity as he is for his attainments, he has, during the five years that I have known him, and that too most intimately and confidentially, pursued his arduous task of endeavouring to improve his countrymen, to beat down superstition, and to hasten as much as possible those reforms in the religion and government of his native land of which both stand in almost equal need. He has done all this, to the great detriment of his private interests, being rewarded by the coldness and jealousy of all the great functionaries of Church and State in India, and supporting the Unitarian Chapel—the Unitarian Press—and the expense of his own publications, besides other charitable acts, out of a private fortune, of which he devotes more than one-third to acts of the purest philanthropy and benevolence.

"I am ready to meet any man living and confirm verbally what I here commit to writing for your use; for nothing will delight me more than to do justice to one whom I honour and esteem as I do this excellent Indian Christian and philosopher." *

The progress made by RAMMOHUN ROY in drawing attention to liberal Christianity attracted considerable attention in the United States, and the Rev. Dr. WARE, Professor of Divinity in Harvard College, addressed a number of questions to him and to Mr. ADAM respecting the best method of promoting the cause of Christianity in

* "Monthly Repository," 1823 Vol. XVIII., p 442.

India. Replies were made to these at considerable length and published.

The following are extracts from the correspondence. In RAMMOHUN ROY's letter to Dr. WARE, dated Calcutta, Feb. 2, 1824, is the following characteristic passage :—

"I have now prepared such replies to those queries as my knowledge authorizes and my conscience permits ; and now submit them to your judgment. There is one question at the concluding part of your letter (to wit, 'Whether it be desirable that the inhabitants of India should be converted to Christianity ; in what degree desirable, and for what reasons ?') which I pause to answer, as I am led to believe, from reason, what is set forth in scripture, that 'in every nation he that *feareth* God and worketh *righteousness* is accepted with him,' in whatever form of worship he may have been taught to glorify God. Nevertheless, I presume to think, that Christianity, if properly inculcated, has a greater tendency to improve the moral, social and political state of mankind, than any other religious system."—*Corresp.*, p p. 125, 129.

The following passages are from his replies :—

"The chief causes which prevent the natives of India from changing their religion, are the same as are found in the numerous class of Christians who are unable to give an answer to any man that asketh the reason of the hope they profess, viz., their reliance on the sanctity of the books received among them as revealed authorities, and the variety of prejudices planted in their minds in the early part of life. These are strongly supported by the dread of the loss of caste, the consequence of apostacy, which separates a husband from his wife, a father from his son, and a mother from her daughter. Besides, the doctrines which the Missionaries mantain and preach are less conformable with reason than those professed by Moosulmans, and in several points are equally absurd with the popular Hindoo creed. Hence there is no rational inducement for either of these tribes to lay aside their respective doctrines, and adopt those held up by the generality of Christians." —*Corresp.*, p. 134.

"Unitarian Christianity is not exposed to the last-mentioned objections; for even those who are inimical to every religion admit that the Unitarian system is more conformable to the human understanding than any other known creed. But the other obstacles above-mentioned must remain unshaken, until the natives are enabled by the diffusion of knowledge to estimate, by comparing one religion with another, their respective merits and advantages, and to relinquish their divisions, as destructive of national union as of social enjoyment.—*Corresp.*, p. 134.

It is probable that many English friends of enlightenment had put themselves into communication with the Hindoo Reformer before his arrival in England. The length of time which has elapsed since his death makes it very difficult to discover traces of the correspondence which doubtless took place between them and him. The following letter to the late J. B. ESTLIN, Esq., of Bristol, for which we are indebted to his daughter, will be read with interest :—

"DEAR SIR,—Mrs. MATTHEW being about to depart for Europe, has kindly offered to take charge of any letter or pamphlet that I may address to you. I embrace this opportunity of acknowledging the receipt of your letter and of the books, your excellent father's Lectures on Moral Philosophy, &c., which I had the honor to receive through Mrs. MATTHEW upwards of two years ago, and apologizing to you for the delay which has unavoidably taken place in answering your kind communication. For a period of more than two years, owing to the most affecting circumstances arising from the hostile feelings of some individuals towards my family, I found myself totally unable to pursue any undertaking or carry on correspondence, even with those whom I